The Substitute

A Survival Manual for the Inexperienced,
Unprepared, or Unmotivated Teacher

JASON W. DAY, BHKin, BEd

EDITED BY R.C. JOSEPH

Trafford
PUBLISHING®   www.trafford.com
North America & international
toll-free: 1 888 232 4444 (USA & Canada)
fax: 812 355 4082

This is for RUBY

Contents

UNIT 4 – LOGIC

UNIT 5 – QUOTATIONS

Introduction

I got the idea to write this survival manual during my first weeks of substitute teaching. I realized very quickly that not all teachers who request a replacement leave materials for the sub to use. Many teachers assume that the sub will use his or her own "tricks of the trade" to keep the students occupied for the duration of class. As a new teacher, I hadn't yet developed any "tricks of the trade." I decided to look for some fun and easy resources to help me since my first experiences in the classroom as a sub were, shall we say, less than encouraging. To my disbelief, I could not find a fun and entertaining resource written with the substitute teacher in mind. So, I wrote one myself!

Each year there are new crops of potential teachers who graduate from university with the daunting task of becoming a substitute teacher. I have experienced some negative situations because, 1) I was inexperienced, 2) I was unprepared, and at times 3) I was unmotivated. With the help of this manual, I believe most teachers will be able to minimize the impact of theses three factors as they gradually become more comfortable with their role as a substitute teacher. Teachers are always looking for resources to add to their collection, and I think this is a perfect one to start with.

UNIT 1
Ice Breakers

1.1 Student Questionnaire

People realize that if there is nothing to do, or their regular teacher hasn't left any work for them, they can make a substitute's life miserable. I experienced this quite a few times, so I started lying to the students! (Hey... whatever gets you through the day) I made up this story:

I tell the students that I am taking a Psychology course at the University and I am compiling information from all of the schools that I visit. I tell them that since I encounter so many students from different schools throughout a week, it gives me an opportunity to get a wide range of data. I ask them if they will help me by filling out an anonymous questionnaire. I explain that some of the questions may be personal, so an anonymous answer sheet is of the utmost importance. I do, however, require their age and gender. (This makes it all sound legit and will help stimulate discussion later) The majority of students are pleased to help me with my "homework." They feel a connection because they see the teacher as a student too. This activity will stimulate a great deal of conversation.

LIFE QUESTIONS — Section A

1. Do you know what you want to do for a living? If so, what?

2. Do you plan to attend university, college, or a vocational school? If so, which one?

3. If you know what you want to do for a living, do you know how to accomplish those goals? Eg. Pilot — Flight school or Air force.

4. Do you expect to change careers throughout your lifetime? If so, how many times?

5. Who can you approach to find out more about a specific career?

6. Do you have a job right now? If so, what?

7. If you work, what is your hourly wage?

8. What wage would you be happy with? Give reasons.

9. How often do you work? What hours do you work?
   Eg: only weekends, after school, etc.

LIFE QUESTIONS — Section B

1. Have you ever drunk alcohol?
2. Have you ever bought alcohol illegally?
3. Have you ever smoked marijuana?
4. Have you ever experimented with any other illegal drug? If so, what?
5. Have you ever puked because of too much alcohol?
6. Have you ever taken someone to the hospital? If so, did you know where to go? Who to talk to?
7. Do you own a car?
8. Have you ever driven over the speed limit? If so, by how much?
9. Have you ever had sex? If so, was it safe sex?
10. Have you ever cheated on a test?

AWARENESS QUESTIONS — Section A

1. How many hours a week do you watch TV?
2. How many TV's are in your house?
3. What are your two favorite TV shows?
4. What are two TV shows that you never watch?
5. How many CD's do you own?
6. What is your favorite song?
7. What is your favorite musical group or performer?
8. What radio stations do you listen to?
9. Do you read the newspaper? If so, what section do you read first?

AWARENESS QUESTIONS — Section B

1. Do you get an allowance from your parents? If so, how much?
2. Do you have a bank account? If so, what kind?
3. What do you spend your money on?
4. Do you have a job? If so, name it.
5. Do you work around the house for money?

AWARENESS QUESTIONS — Section C

1. Do you eat breakfast every morning?
2. Do you follow a regular exercise routine?
3. What time do you go to bed on a school night?
4. What time do you go to bed on the weekends?
5. How much time do you spend on homework on a weekly basis?
6. What do you usually do on Saturday afternoons?
7. Do you use the snooze button on your alarm clock?

AWARENESS QUESTIONS — Section D

1. What is the first thing you do when you get home from school?
2. Who prepares your lunch for school?
3. Do you have any brothers or sisters? How many?
4. How many adults do you live with?
5. Who cleans your bedroom?
6. Who cleans the dishes?
7. Who makes dinner?
8. Who makes your bed?
9. Who eats dinner at the dinner table?
10. Do you own any pets?
11. Who feeds them?
12. Do you have a TV in your bedroom?
13. Do you share a bedroom?

1.2 How did you know that?

Leave instructions on the board. Ask the students to take out a scrap piece of paper. Read out the following questions and have the students write down the answer as quickly as they can.

What is?

1 + 5?

2 + 4?

3 + 3?

4 + 2?

5 + 1?

Tell the students to repeat the answer (6) in their head as fast as they can for 10 seconds.

Ask the students to write down the answer to the following question. Please do it quietly.

What is the first vegetable that comes to mind?

Tell them that the vegetable they are thinking of is a CARROT!

1.3 What would you do?
1 in 100 chance to win $1000.

As a teacher, one can always encourage a personal financial strategy. If you are prepared, the visual aspect of this exercise hits home. I came to class with photocopied $5, $10, $20 bills. I had a stack of them, but they were obviously fake. I suggest that you make yours obviously fake as well so as not to encourage any illegal activity. (One suggestion that worked was replacing the picture of the person on the particular bill with a picture of yourself. This usually gets a good reaction.) The concept of the exercise is to give the students a choice. The students who win the game can even buy a prize from you with their fake money. (Make sure you come prepared with little prizes or candies)

Tell the students that they will be given $10 and that they will have an opportunity to play a game of chance. Put the overhead of the next page up on the screen. Let all the students see what their chances are and ask each individual what they would choose. By a show of hands, ask the students who would choose the first option. Have them take out a scrap piece of paper and write down a number. If anyone guesses the same number as you have, count out $1000 to that student. In my experience, it has only happened once, but the roar of the classroom was music to my ears. The students were having fun and some even told me they would never forget this class. Obviously you can do the same procedure with the rest of the options. Every time someone wins, the classroom usually gets quite loud. This one is a lot of fun!

Questions to ponder:

Is this gambling? When is gambling fun? When is it not? What is compound interest? What are long term financial goals? Are they fool proof? Should you ever take a risk? If so, at what cost? Etc.

#1

A chance of winning,
1 in 100. If you win you get
$1000

#2

You decide not to play at all.
You keep the $10

#3

A chance of winning,
1 in 2. If you win
you get $20

#4

A chance of winning,
1 in 5. If you win
you get $50

1.4 Why worry? Only 2 things to worry about.

Yet another ice breaker. Put this on the overhead when you first get into class. It is always nice to start a class with something funny or interesting. I got this from the wall of a restaurant bathroom. You never know where you'll find something of interest or of some educational value.

In life there are only 2 things to worry about:

Either you are well or you are sick.

If you are well, there's nothing to worry about.

If you are sick, there are only 2 things to worry about:

Either you get better or you die.

If you get better, there's nothing to worry about.

If you die, there are only 2 things to worry about:

Either you go to HEAVEN or you go to HELL.

If you go to HEAVEN, there's nothing to worry about.

If you go to HELL, you'll be so damn busy shaking hands with friends from Mr. Bergstrom's class that YOU'LL HAVE NO TIME TO WORRY!

1.5 Good attitude, Bad attitude

Like so many of us, a student's attitude is constantly being scrutinized throughout their school career. How many times have you heard a teacher say that they didn't like a particular student's attitude? Conversely, good attitudes are widely praised by teachers. Truthfully, the students with the bad attitudes are the ones that you usually remember. The point of this exercise is to allow students to discuss and understand what good and bad attitudes really are.

This activity is quite simple.

- Write the word 'ATTITUDE' on the board in big bold letters.

- Ask the students to write down as many words that come to mind when they see this word.

- Give them 3 minutes or so to complete this task. (Sometimes groups can work together, but I have found that doing this task individually works best.)

- Next, ask them to define the word as best they can. This is a good time for discussion.

- Poll the class. See how many students use positive words when defining or describing the word 'attitude'. Ask to see who uses negative words when defining and describing the word 'attitude'.

Questions to ponder:

Why do some people automatically consider the word 'attitude' to be positive? negative? What forces can control this? (eg. Radio, television, schools, home, etc.) What are some situations in life where a 'good attitude' can be beneficial? When is a 'bad attitude' beneficial? (Go back to the words that were used when asked to describe a 'bad attitude') Ask the students who consider themselves to have a good attitude/bad attitude? Why? What are the positives and negatives of both?

1.6 Time = $86,400

I make a transparency of this story and start a class with it!

Imagine there is a bank that credits your account each morning with $86,400. It carries over no balance from day to day. Every evening it deletes whatever part of the balance you failed to use during the day.

What would you do?

Draw out every cent, of course!

Each of us has such a bank. It's name is TIME. Every morning, it credits you with 86,400 seconds.

Every night it writes off, as cost, whatever of this you have failed to invest to good use. Carries over no balance. It allows no overdraft. Each day it opens a new account for you. Each night it burns the remains of the day. If you fail to use the day's deposits, the loss is yours. There is no going back. There is no drawing against the "tomorrow." You must live in the present on today's deposits. Invest it so as to get from it the utmost in health, happiness, and success! The clock is running.

MAKE THE MOST OF TODAY. To realize the value of ONE YEAR, ask a student who failed a grade. To realize the value of ONE MONTH, ask a mother who gave birth to a premature baby. To realize the value of ONE WEEK, ask the editor of a weekly newspaper. To realize the value of ONE HOUR, ask the lovers who are waiting to meet. To realize the value of ONE MINUTE, ask a person who missed their flight. To realize the value of ONE SECOND, ask a person who just avoided an accident. To realize the value of ONE MILLISECOND, ask the person who won a silver medal in the winter Olympics.

Treasure every moment that you have! And remember that time waits for no one.

Yesterday is history. Tomorrow is mystery. Today is a gift.

Author: unknown

1.7 Is it only Rock and Roll?

Keeping it fun and light, this one takes just a few seconds to set up.

Ask students to list as many TYPES of music as they can. The purpose of this exercise is to make them aware of the numerous kinds of music and that "their" type of music is not the only one. Other people in the world will find different types of music cool. Encourage students not to judge people by what type of music they listen to.

After finding out how many types of music a few students compiled, put this list up on the overhead. I would assume that no one got close to this amount.

Questions to ponder:

Who or what do you associate with a type of music? eg. Elevator music = old people. Challenge students to seek out these different types of music and listen to it for a week. Was it enjoyable? Did you learn something? Were you apprehensive to tell people what type of music you were listening to? Why? Is it necessary to categorize music? (alternative vs. rock?) etc.

This list comes from the Archive of Contemporary Music in New York City.

a cappella	juju
acid	mariachi
acid rock	meringue
Afro beat	minimal
Ambient	Motown
Apala	new age
Avant-garde	new wave
Blues	noise music
Bluebeat	northern soul
Blue-eyed soul	oi!
Bolero	palm wine
British invasion	polka

Bubble gum	power pop
Bugaloo	protest
Cadence	psychedelic
Cajun	pub rock
Calypso	punk
Charanga	punta
Computer	rai
Country swing	rap
Cumbia	rebel rock
Dance music	reggae
Disco	rhythm and blues
Doo-wop	rock and roll
Dub	rock opera
Electro pop	rockabilly
Electronic	rock steady
Film and tv music	salsa
Flamenco	samba
Folk rock	San Francisco sound
Fuji	ska
Funk	skiffle
Fusion	skinhead
Garage	soca
Glam and glitter rock	soft rock
Go-go	soukous
Gospel	soul
Griot	speed metal
Gypsy	steel band
Hardcore	surf
Heavy metal	tex-mex
High energy	tex swing
Hip hop	toasting

1.8 Things to do in an elevator.

Entertaining to say the least!

1. When people get on, ask for their tickets.
2. When there's only one other person in the elevator, tap them on the shoulder and then pretend it wasn't you.
3. Push the buttons and pretend they give you a shock. Smile and go back for more.
4. Hold the doors open and say you're waiting for your friend. After a while, let the doors close and say, "Hey Jimbo! What be happenin'?"
5. Constantly bounce a basketball.
6. Drop a quarter and wait until someone reaches to help pick it up, say "that's mine!"
7. Stand in the corner reading the yellow pages, giggling.
8. Take pictures of everyone in the elevator.
9. When the doors close, announce to the others, "Its okay. They'll open up again."
10. Push your floor button with your elbow.
11. Stand alone, and when the doors open tell people trying to get on that the car is full and that they should wait for the next one.
12. Swat at flies that don't exist.
13. Wink at everyone who gets on.
14. Introduce yourself to everyone who gets on the elevator. "Hello, my name is Sanmar and I am very pleased to have this ride with you."

1.9 Who, what, where?

Another test for your students. Stress to the class that they must complete each step in their head. Do not answer out loud or it will spoil the effect.

THINK of a number from 1 to 10.

MULTIPLY that number by 9.

If the number is a 2-digit number, ADD the digits together.

Now SUBTRACT 5.

DETERMINE which letter in the alphabet corresponds to the number you ended up with (example: 1=a, 2=b, 3=c, etc.)

THINK of a country that starts with that letter. REMEMBER the last letter of the name of that country.

THINK of the name of an animal that starts with that letter.

REMEMBER the last letter in the name of that animal.

THINK of the name of a fruit that starts with that letter.

Are you thinking of a *Kangaroo in Denmark eating an Orange*?!

1.10 The missing 'F' sentence

Choose to either write this sentence on the board, or make an overhead of this sheet. Instruct the students to do this activity on their own.

Read this sentence only once:

FINISHED FILES ARE THE RE-
SULT OF YEARS OF SCIENTIF-
IC STUDY COMBINED WITH
THE EXPERIENCE OF YEARS.

Now count the F's in the sentence. Write your answer down on a piece of paper.

ANSWER:

There are six F's in the sentence. Many people forget the "OF"'s. The human brain tends to see them as V's and not F's.

1.11 Card Tricks

Having a card trick can be a great ice breaker. If you would like to introduce yourself this way, or if you have some extra time at the end of the class, card tricks can be a fun way to entertain. I found that some of the kids in the class have a trick or two that they would like to show as well. It is always fun to trick the students, but I found that they love it when you show them how to do it. I know it is a 'cardinal sin' to reveal the method of magic tricks, but after all, aren't we in the business of teaching children, rather than leaving them in the dark. Who knows, you might encourage a budding new magician to perfect his trade.

Here are some examples of easy card tricks that you can use. Depending on your personality, you may want to graduate to some more mind boggling ones, but for the sake of this manual, I think these will do the "trick."

Trick #1

Do the first 3 steps away from your audience.

1) Take the four Kings out of the deck, and also two other cards.

2) Fan the four Kings out, and place the two other cards you selected behind the second King. Line them up so your audience cannot see the two other cards.

3) Show the Kings to the class.

4) Place the Kings (and the two secret cards) face down on the top of the deck.

5) Tell the audience that the four Kings are good friends, and they don't let anything get between them.

6) Place the top King on the bottom of the deck. You may show the class this card.

7) Place the next card (not a King) into the center of the deck.

8) Repeat step 7.

9) Leave the fourth card on the top. You may show the class that it is a King.

10) Explain that the Kings are real good friends and will soon be back together.

11) Cut the deck in the middle, and put the bottom half on the top.

12) Search the deck for the four Kings. They have been magically moved next to each other.

Trick #2

The Show: With a class member's help, make four piles of cards. When this is done you flip over all the piles and all four Aces are there.

Preparation: Arrange the deck like so: three Aces on the bottom and one on the top.

Presentation: Ask the student to tell you when to stop putting down cards. Begin dealing cards face down on the table. Continue until they have you stop. After the first pile is down, stick the card deck, still in your hand, under the table and put the bottom card on top. This gives you an Ace on the top. Repeat the above steps until you have four piles. Then flip over all the piles to show an Ace on the bottom of each!

Trick #3

The Show: Deck is shuffled, and a student cuts it in half. The student chooses one cut portion and performer takes the other. Both student and performer hold cards behind their back and select a card. The cards selected are then exchanged and placed face up behind the back. This is repeated one more time. When done, both people bring out their pile and spread them out. All four Two's will be face up.

Preparation: Put the four Two's in your back pocket. Do this where no one can see you.

Card Trick:

1) Shuffle deck. Let student cut in half and choose a pile; you take the other pile.

2) Tell the student to do exactly what you do.

3) Put cards behind back, have the student do the same.

(You secretly take the four Two's from your pocket and put them on the top of your pile.)

4) Both of you select a card (you pick the top Two).

5) Then you exchange cards without looking at them.

6) Tell the student to put it behind her back, face up, anywhere in the deck.

7) As she does this, put the student's card on the bottom of your pile, take a Two from the top and put it face up anywhere.

8) Repeat steps 4-7 one more time.

9) Then bring the cards out. Join the two halves together. Spread the cards to show all four Two's face up!

1.12 Classroom Baseball/Football/ Jeopardy

Always be prepared. I keep two "noise makers" in my bag of tricks. Something that is not overly loud usually makes for a good buzzer. Dollar stores are a great place to find fun and quirky noise makers.

I would assume that the TV game shows "Jeopardy" and "Family Feud" are easily explained to the class. Making sure that you have a way of distinguishing different sounds is most important for the teacher. (Then you won't have to deal with some kids cheating or saying that they rang in first). All three of these games require some work on the students' part. Ask the students to come up with some questions that pertain to the area of study that they are involved with right now. Groups work well here. Make sure to have the students produce easy questions as well as harder questions. Set the games up as if you were playing "Jeopardy" or "Family Feud." You will be the game show host asking all of the questions. Your decisions are final.

As for Classroom Baseball, you have to make some alterations to the classroom. This is kind of fun, since the kids get to move their desks around and make a large open space in the middle of the room. Make a baseball field. Use a chair or desk or prop in the room to make the bases. The questions that the students come up with should be labeled as either a single, double, triple or home run. Obviously the easier questions are going to be singles and the harder ones are home runs. Play as if you were playing baseball. Eg. Three outs means the other team gets to "bat."

1.13 Tongue Twisters

Many students will have their own tongue twisters to share!

Greek grapes.

Which wristwatches are Swiss wristwatches?

Unique New York.

Freshly-fried flying fish.

The epitome of femininity.

A skunk sat on a stump and thunk the stump stunk, but the stump thunk the skunk stunk.

She stood on the balcony, inexplicably mimicing him hiccupping, and amicably welcoming him home.

She sells seashells by the seashore.
The shells she sells are surely seashells.
So if she sells shells on the seashore,
I'm sure she sells seashore shells.

Peter Piper picked a peck of pickled peppers.
Did Peter Piper pick a peck of pickled peppers?
If Peter Piper Picked a peck of pickled peppers,
Where's the peck of pickled peppers Peter Piper picked?

How much wood would a woodchuck chuck
If a woodchuck could chuck wood?
He would chuck, he would, as much as he could,
And chuck as much as a woodchuck would
If a woodchuck could chuck wood.

I'm not a smart feller,
I'm a smart feller's son
And I'll keep felling smarts
'Till the smart feller comes

1.14 Bar Tricks

Play with these until you are somewhat competent at performing the trick.

Trick #1

SET UP – Always carry a book of matches. Pull one match from the book of matches. Usually, matches have two different colors on either side of the match. Tell the students that the black side will represent "heads" and the cardboard side will represent "tails." Tell the students that you will toss the match in the air and if the match lands on either "heads" or "tails" they win and you will buy them all a candy bar. Then tell them, if the match lands on its side, you win and they have to finish their work, or be quiet, or whatever else you see fit. (Sometimes a candy bar is just as good.)

HOW IT'S DONE – You will probably get a few groans from the kids after you've done this, but it works. Take the match in your fingers and bend it in half. 99% of the time, when you throw it in the air, it will land on its' side. There you have it. A fool proof way to win a bet!

Trick #2

SET UP – For this trick, you will need a brandy snifter and a marble. In the bar we use a stemless cherry or an olive, but a marble will do. Place the marble on a table and then place the brandy snifter over top of the marble. The snifter should be upside down, over top the marble. Ask the students to try and get the brandy snifter to be right side up with the marble inside without touching anything other than the brandy snifter.

HOW IT'S DONE – the concept of Centrifical Force is used. If you take the brandy snifter and rotate it in a circular motion, the marble will move around the inside of the glass. Once you have the marble moving, you can turn the snifter right side up and have the marble inside.

HINT – if you can't turn the snifter right side up, try and place the marble into another container. The concept

is the same, move the snifter in a circular motion, but instead of turning the snifter right side up, lift the snifter over another container, slow down your circular motion, and drop the marble into the other container. Touch nothing except the brandy snifter.

Trick #3

SET UP – This trick is a good one because you can use a five dollar bill as incentive. You will need three pieces of equipment. Since you will be in a school classroom, I suggest that you use a glass pop bottle, rather than a beer bottle. Either kind of bottle will work. Next, place a crisp $5 bill on top of the bottle. Now, on top of the $5 bill, place a quarter. Ask a student to try and remove the $5 bill while keeping the quarter balanced on top of the bottle. The only rule is the only piece of equipment that can be touched is the $5 bill.

HOW IT'S DONE – For best results, use a crisp bill. Next, when placing the bill on the bottle, move the bill down to one side. In other words, don't place the bill in the middle, stagger it a bit on top of the bottle. Now, with the quarter balanced on top of the bill, lick you index finger and quickly and firmly wack down on the $5 bill. You should try and hit it as close to the bottle as possible. You may want to hold onto the bottle with your other hand, just to stabilize it. With practice, the $5 bill will slide out from under the quarter, leaving it balanced on top of the bottle.

Trick #4

SET UP – This trick is a little easier to figure out. All you need are 6 containers. They do not need to be very big, just big enough to hold some liquid. In the bar we use shot glasses. Fill 3 of the containers with water. Place all six containers in a row with the ones filled with water in the first, second and third positions. Ask a student, by only moving one container, have the containers alternate from full, empty, full, empty and so on.

HOW IT'S DONE – Pick up the second container and empty its contents into the fifth container. Now the containers alternate from full to empty, full, empty.

Trick #5

SET UP – All you need is one glass, usually we use a pint glass, but any glass will do and two quarters. Place both quarters on the rim of the glass opposite from each other. Ask a student to remove both quarters from the glass without touching anything other than the quarters. You are only allowed to use your index finger and thumb of one hand.

HOW IT'S DONE – Carefully slide one quarter around the rim of the glass so it is beside the other quarter. Using your index finger and thumb, pinch the outside of one quarter with your index finger and pinch the outside of the other quarter with your thumb. Quickly lift up and both quarters will end up in your hand.

These are only a few tricks that I have learned along the way. There are plenty of web sites with great ideas and other tricks to learn. Once you bring out one trick, the students are going to remember you, so you better be prepared for keeping them entertained!

1.15 Shish Kabob

Impress the students with these 3 games!

Visual Recognition

This is a quick and easy game to play. It utilizes all of the materials that you have in your bag of tricks. The idea is to lay out 30 assorted small items on a desk and cover them with a cloth. Show them to the class for 2 minutes. Re-cover all of the materials and have the students write down as many as they can remember. I like to stress that there needs to be quiet in the room for this game to work. It's always fun to see the student's faces when they see the items that they missed.

Hand signals

First of all, students must sit in a circle so that every student can see each other. Next, each student chooses a hand signal for themselves and demonstrates it to the rest of the class. Inevitably you will get some inappropriate gestures, but depending on the class, I will let it go. The bad ones get taken early and if you have a larger class, the gestures usually get quite creative. The game starts by choosing one student to give their sign and the sign of another student. The other student must recognize their sign and reply by giving the sign of another student. Hopefully this sequence goes on for awhile. You are out of the game if you fail to recognize your own sign or give a sign of someone who is already out of the game. Everyone stays involved in the circle by looking for others who make mistakes. To restart the game, the student who sent the signal to the person who is out sends another signal.

Shish kabob

This is an enjoyable game 'right off the bat' since the title is so fun. Ask each student to write a verb or action word down on a piece of paper. Tell them to keep it to themselves. Choose a student to answer "yes" or "no" to questions about their verb. Students take turns asking questions in the form of replacing the verb with the words "shish kabob." For example, "Do you shish kabob only at night?" Each student is only allowed one guess at what the actual activity is. If they get it right, they are up next.

UNIT 2
Visuals

2.1 Optical illusions

Optical illusions are always fun. This is a great
opportunity to discuss that sometimes, things aren't
always as they appear. Sometimes, greater thought or
analysis is needed to understand the entire picture.

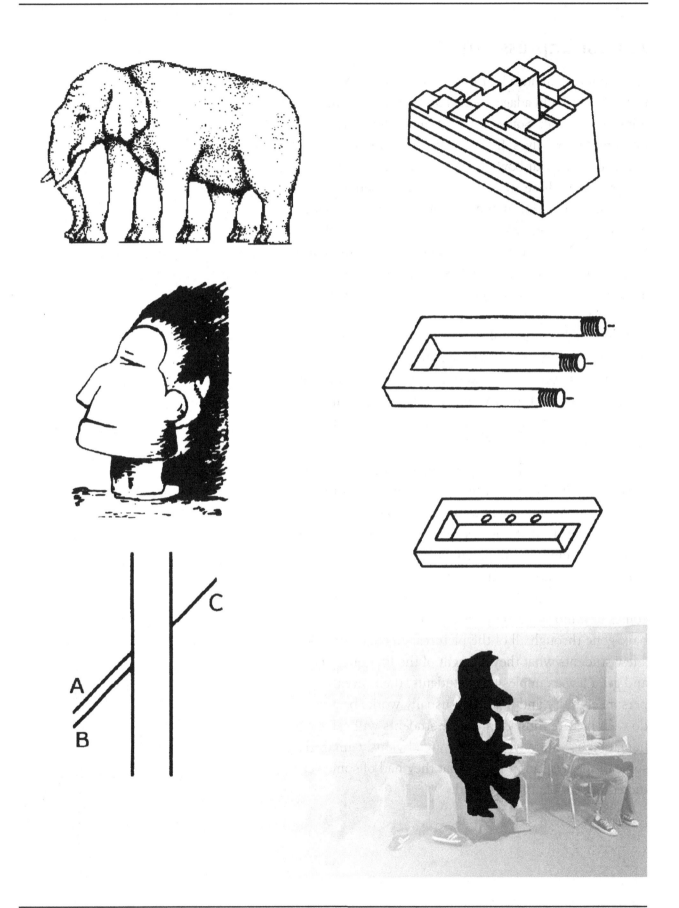

2.2 First impressions

Never underestimate a first impression. This activity tackles the age old adage, "you can never make a first impression twice." Sometimes first impressions are very important in our lives. If you are going on a job interview, or are meeting your boyfriend, or girlfriend's parents for the first time. These are times in your life where your appearance and demeanor are scrutinized first. As with most things in life, there are always two sides to every story. What I think is important here is to help students understand that first impressions are not always true. Sometimes people can deceive us into thinking that they are who they appear to be. We must make wise and informed decisions about the people with whom we have relationships. This exercise may be exaggerated, but hopefully it encourages youngsters to stop and think before making decisions. While first impressions are important in most aspects of life, they can also be used to create false impressions which can be harmful.

You will need to find some pictures from the internet to complete this activity. I have listed ten interesting people who you may want to use. Look them up and see what you think. Show the class one picture at a time and allow them to write down what they think of the person in the photograph. Short, quick answers will be best. Encourage them to write down what initially comes to mind when they see this person. Once you have gone through all of the pictures, go back and ask a few students what they thought of the first one. Try and get a few examples from students, then reveal the persons identity and history. It usually works best if you do each picture individually. The students will get the hang of it as you move on. They are obviously amazed at some of the first impressions that they had of some very incredible people in this world.

First impressions answer key

JESSE OWENS: famous for winning an unprecedented 4 gold medals at the 1936 Berlin Olympic Games.

FIDEL CASTRO: has been the president of Cuba since 1959.

PAMELA SMART: a school teacher who was convicted of masterminding a plot to kill her husband. She coerced a young student of her's to
do the killing.

MARY SHADD CARY: an editor and civil rights advocate. First black woman in North America to edit a newspaper.

ALBERT EINSTEIN: inventor, scientist, mathematician, and most famous for his theory of relativity.

ORVILLE AND WILBUR WRIGHT: the Wright Brothers invented the airplane and were the first to take flight.

LEE HARVEY OSWALD: was accused of assassinating President John F. Kennedy. Was later assassinated himself.

EVA BRAUN: Hitler's girlfriend and later wife, just before they both died.

NEIL YOUNG: famous Canadian singer song writer.

JOHN WAYNE GACY: convicted serial killer who buried his victims under the floor boards in his own home. 30+ victims.

2.3 Nine Toothpick Problems

I gathered these brainteasers over the years from teachers, as well as some of my students. Here are the instructions for problems.

1. By moving only 2 sticks and keeping the general shape of them, (the shape resembles a football upright) have the circle appear on the outside of the upright.

2. By using only one "stroke," make this statement true.

3. By moving only one stick, make this statement true.

4. By moving only one stick, make this statement true.

5. Starting at the top right dot, connect all of the other nine dots with only 4 straight lines. The 4 lines must all be connected and your pencil can not leave the paper while drawing.

6. By moving only 3 dots, make this image upside down. Hint – the peak of the triangle should be pointing down when you are finished.

7. Create this image without ever crossing your own line. You have to be careful when watching to see if the students cross their own lines.

8. Move 4 sticks from this pattern to leave 3 squares.

9. Move 2 sticks in order to make 11 squares.

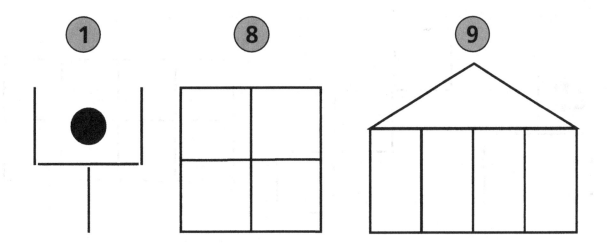

(1) (8) (9)

(2) **5 + 5 + 5 = 550**

(3) $IX - XII = III$

(4) $\dfrac{I}{VII}$

(7)

(5)

(6)

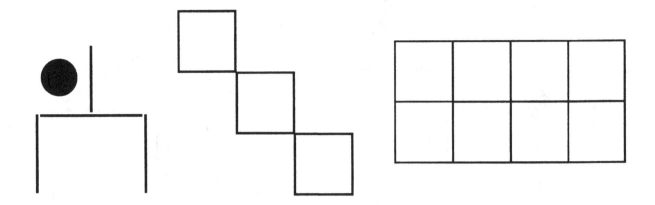

5 4 5 + 5 = 550

$$IX = XII - III$$

$$\frac{I}{\sqrt{I}}$$

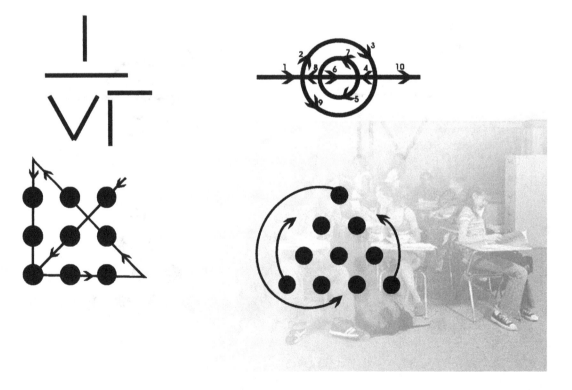

2.4 Scribble Art

I got this idea from a student who was talking about how to waste time while on a long car trip. My wife's parents always said, "Go to sleep, the time goes by faster." The typical cry from the back seat in my family car was, "Are we there yet?!" Some people have great ideas to pass the time in the car, but I was always trying to get the last punch in on my brother before my Dad told us to quit, or he would "pull over right now and make us both walk home." Other people would count red cars or the number of wheels on big semi trucks, while others would play "pididdle." This was when driving at night, if you could spot a car with only one head light, you would yell out, Pididdle! If you were correct you got a point, but if you were incorrect, because the car turned out to be, a motor-cycle, you would lose a point.

Activity: Ask the students to scribble anything down on a piece of paper. You may have to demonstrate on the board, but scribble down anything that at least uses only one line which is simple and has shape. Instruct the students to thoughtfully look at the scribble and then add lines to make the scribble into something else. You may want to try more than one scribble and see what the students come up with. You may also want to have one student scribble, and then pass it to a friend and see what they can create. Finally, you could put a scribble on the board, and ask each student to create something from it. Have them come up to the board and re-create their image and compare and contrast them with the other students.

2.5 **Triangle Test**

This structure consists of nine equally sized triangles. Remove four of the lines (between the dots) so that you are left with five equal sized triangles.

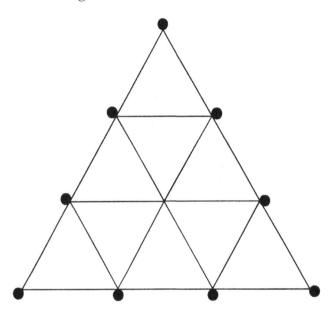

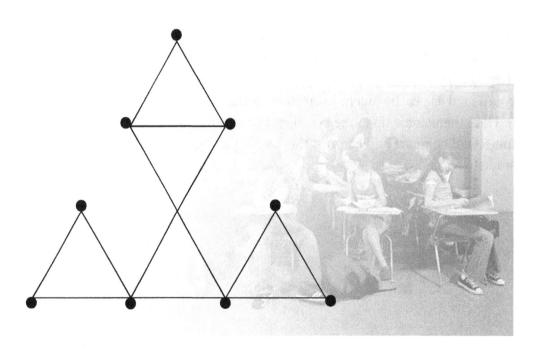

2.6 Word Search

Word search puzzles have always been a fun way of passing time. Sometimes you need an activity that is just plain fun. These puzzles are a great way to keep students occupied for a few moments. If the regular teacher has left work for the students to complete, these puzzles are an extra way to keep the students on task. Inevitably, some kids will finish the assigned work before the end of class. If you can incorporate your word puzzles into the regular teacher's assigned work, the kids won't know the difference. Have fun with these puzzles. They may come in handy one day.

Hint: It is always nice to have some photocopies of these in your bag of tricks. You never know when you may need them.

Find each of the following words.

STAGE	AMP	TRAVEL	BASS
ROADIE	BARBAND	MACHINEHEAD	GUITAR
DRUMS	CHORD	TREBLECLEF	ROCKSTAR
SHOULDERSTRAP	COWBELL	KEYBOARD	
FRET	TUNER	GIG	
NOTE	STUDIO	PICK	

```
K R T R D R E D P T R E B L E C L E F A W C L
N D M R E C A U T G H A E L A A L T D R F T R
E A U S A A E U B R L F V E L D A S O A L N D
D E D E G V T E O O R R E N U T T T B S A A I
C H E R W S E D E N R A R G D U A A R T L A O
H E N E O A D L E I E L T B D R D R E R B T T
O N A T U H E L R R I D L I W D A R R L A F S
R I D O U A C R D I D S O E U E R O E S S Y I
M H U N E O S G E A A T A S B G T U B C S C S
F C S B A R B A N D O A R O R W S I M Y L R D
O A G I E E D E Y Y R G R O C B O A E S E L A
U M I I A K H M P C T E D L D E A C D L S K C
K I G K O N U A D F O G E A M P R C L T R B G
R R U A B G K C I P R O C K S T A R P W I W S
P A R T S R E D L U O H S O K U R D F R E T U
L U O S U O A E E N O A A S D I G A R G T O I
```

Find each of the following words.

ROTTENEGGS   PASSGAS   CHEESER   PANTSPUFFER
RIPONE   POOGAS   GASSER   RIPSNORTER
BEEF   BACKBLAST   LETONEFLY   BROWNHAZE
BLAST   CUTTHECHEESE BARKINGSPIDERS STINKER
BOMBERS   AIRBISCUIT   POOF   BREAKWIND

```
R S R E D I P S G N I K R A B P H E O H C D T
R A S W O E W W E U P G S E H O O S O Y R N A
B T I U C S I B R I A I K E P O T T E N G I I
L C S S M E H P S T I N K E R F B E E F O W B
A I R S C E Z A O P A N T S P U F F E R T K P
S Y E R S H I A F O E N O P I R G R B E G A R
T L T S A C S N H T G N T S B S N A L M R E E
R E A S E A N G N F A S S R G R S S R E R P
I E F G U H W R P C W B S P A E E R A S N B E
C N I S R T B H R U S O T R B L S G T L E C A
C O R S N T U I H S N R B S U B E G S A R D
R T L A B U R B E S B O M B E R S K E F G C S
D E N P B C R S R I P S N O R T E R C H B D I
P L E B I R O T T E N E G G S B B E S A C R R
I I I C L L N S D A P I S G E H E S P E B R S
B P T E M F A R O G K E E N N O D T C C T C A
```

UNIT 3
Reasoning

3.1 What are they trying to teach me?

Richard Carlson's book, <u>Don't Sweat the Small Stuff and It's All Small Stuff</u> has some wonderful life lessons that we can all live by. There are a number of ideas that I have used in my daily life and some that I have tried to pass along to the students that I meet. This one caught my eye.

"The idea is to imagine that everyone you know and everyone you meet is perfectly enlightened. That is, everyone except you! The people you meet are all here to teach you something. Perhaps the obnoxious driver or disrespectful teenager is here to teach you about patience, the punk rocker might be here to teach you to be less judgmental. Your job is to try to determine what the people in your life are trying to teach you." (Carlson, p. 31)

The activity is quite simple.

- Write a question on the board or overhead such as: Have you ever encountered a situation in your lifetime where someone has completely frustrated you? If so, please write down the general description of this incident.

- After a reasonable amount of time has been given to answer the question, start discussing the stories.

- What I found is that many of the stories the students come up with are quite amusing. This helps in setting the tone for the class. If funny stories are being told, the students usually have a good time.

- Now that the students are on your side, present to them the idea that everyone in the world is correct, except you! Stress that no matter how absurd the situation was; encourage them to think that they were wrong.

- Ask them now to try and come up with some answers to the question, "What are they trying to teach me?" There is always at least one student who says that there was nothing to learn from their particular experience. Ask them only to IMAGINE that they were wrong.

- Finally, it is interesting to discuss the solutions to each student's situation. You may be amazed at some of the students' ideas. This is when teaching is fun.

3.2 Can you challenge authority?

Pose a simple question to your students. What would happen if we want to challenge authority? Encourage them to think about why there are authority figures and what the actual consequences would be if that authority is challenged. (if any) Also, why are the rules different for some authority figures compared to others?

What happens if we want to challenge:

1. Our parents?

2. Our teacher?

3. Our principal?

4. Police officers?

5. The Government?

6. Revenue Canada?

7. The neighborhood bully?

8. The Mafia?

9. A local gang member?

10. The Hell's Angles?

Please encourage the students to be as realistic as possible. Eg. Is your life in danger if you challenge your mother's authority?

3.3 Shrink the Earth's population

This next piece is an urban legend that has been dated back to the 1950's, author unknown. Even if the data is somewhat outdated, it is fun to discuss the need for education and awareness in our global society.

If we could shrink the Earth's population to a village of exactly 100 people, with all the existing human ratios remaining the same, it would look something like the following:

There would be:

- 57 Asians
- 21 Europeans
- 14 from the Western Hemisphere, both north and south
- 8 Africans

- 52 would be female
- 48 would be male

- 70 would be nonwhite
- 30 would be white

- 70 would be non Christian
- 30 would be Christian

- 89 would be heterosexual
- 11 would be homosexual

- 6 people would possess 59% of the entire world's wealth and all 6 would be from the United States

- 80 would live in substandard housing
- 70 would be unable to read
- 50 would suffer from malnutrition

- 1 would be near death
- 1 would be near birth

- 1 would have a college education
- 1 would own a computer

When one considers our world from such a compressed perspective, the need for acceptance, understanding and education becomes glaringly apparent.

The following is also something to ponder:

If you woke up this morning with more health than illness... you are more blessed than the million who will not survive this week.

If you have never experienced the danger of battle, the loneliness of imprisonment, the agony of torture, or the pangs of starvation... you are ahead of 500 million people in the world.

If you can attend a church meeting without fear of harassment, arrest, torture, or death... you are more blessed than 3 billion people in the world.

If you have food in the refrigerator, clothes on your back, a roof overhead and a place to sleep... you are richer than 75% of this world.

If you have money in the bank, in your wallet, and spare change in a dish somewhere... you are among the world's wealthiest 8%.

If your parents are still alive and still married... you are very rare.

3.4 Remember Columbine

This letter is a good way to remember the tragedy that occurred at Columbine High School in Colorado on April 20, 1999. I think this should be talked about in high school and should not be forgotten. I would suggest you do a little homework yourself about this topic to be able to answer a few of the many questions that you will face.

Here is an excerpt from www.rockymountainnews.com :

On April 20, 1999 two students walked into Columbine High School, fired from multi-gun arsenal and lobbed homemade bombs throughout the school. They killed 12 students and one teacher before committing suicide.

This letter was found on the internet. Its authenticity is not confirmed, but it is interesting reading nonetheless:

The paradox of our time in history is that we have taller buildings, but narrower viewpoints. We spend more, but have less; we buy more, but enjoy it less.

We have bigger houses and smaller families; more conveniences, but less time; we have more degrees, but less sense; more knowledge, but less judgment; more experts, but more problems; more medicine, but less wellness.

We drink too much, smoke too much, spend too recklessly, laugh too little, drive too fast, get too angry too quickly, stay up too late, get up too tired, read too seldom, watch too much TV.

We have multiplied our possessions, but reduced our values, we talk too much, love too seldom, and hate too often. We've learned how to make a living, but not a life; we've added years to life, but not life to years.

We've been all the way to the moon and back, but have trouble crossing the street to meet the new neighbor.

We've conquered outer space, but not inner space. We've done larger things, but not better things. We've cleaned up the air, but polluted the soul. We've split the atom,

but not our prejudice. We plan more, but accomplish less. We've learned to rush, but not to wait.

We build more computers to hold more information to produce more copies than ever, but have less communication. These are the times of fast foods and slow digestion; tall men, and short character; steep profits and shallow relationships. These are the times of world peace, but domestic warfare; more leisure, but less fun; more kinds of food, but less nutrition. These are days of two incomes, but more divorce; of fancier houses, but broken homes; disposable diapers, throwaway morality; one night stands, overweight bodies, and pills that do everything from cheer to quit to kill.

It is a time when there is much in the show window and nothing in the stockroom; a time when technology can bring this letter to you, and a time when you can choose either to share this insight, or to just hit delete. I choose to share it.

3.5 Be prepared for the unexpected

I got the idea for this activity from a personal experience. Late one evening my best friend and I were driving home and we witnessed a horrific traffic accident. A small sports car had crossed the center line and hit a mini van head on. The three passengers in the sports car were flung from their vehicle and lay on the side of the road. We were the first persons on the scene. I must admit that I was not prepared for this experience. On the other hand, my best friend sprang into action without hesitation. It didn't take long for the fire trucks and ambulance to get there, but my friend had taken control of the situation and did his best until the professionals arrived.

I later asked him how he was able to perform under such a stressful situation. His answer was simple… he was prepared. He said that he had thought about this kind of dilemma in his head before, just in case it actually did happen. When it did happen, he felt that he already had experience and was able to do the right things.

I have tried to relate some experiences to the students I teach.

- I go on the assumption that some students are engaging in illegal activities, (eg. underage drinking or smoking pot) and instead of ignoring them, I try to help them by giving them some idea of what could happen in the future.

- These questions could start with, "what would you do if…" or "have you ever…"

- Please use your discretion in both asking and answering these questions.

- Ask the students to keep their written answers anonymous.

ARE YOU PREPARED FOR THE UNEXPECTED?

1. Have you ever driven a car over the speed limit?
2. Have you ever been pulled over by a police officer?
3. Do you know what is expected of you if you are pulled over by a police officer?

4. Have you ever drunk more than 3 alcoholic beverages in one sitting?

5. What would you do if your friend started vomiting after drinking several alcoholic beverages?

6. Have you ever seen someone puke from drinking too much?

7. Have you ever been to a hospital?

8. What would you do if you needed to get to a hospital?

9. Have you ever called 911?

10. Have you ever witnessed a car accident?

11. What would you do if you were the first person on the scene of a terrible car accident?

12. Who would you call in case of an emergency?

3.6 **What do you want to do with your life?**

What I am trying to accomplish with this activity is to use the medium in which school aged children can identify with the most. Music videos. There was one video in particular which I remembered to be quite influential. The video in question is "We're Not Gonna Take It" by Twisted Sister. The simple storyline of the video is a young kid who has a disciplinarian father and a timid, stereotypical '50's stay at home mom. The father obviously hates the music which is coming from the young boy's bedroom, and goes upstairs to set the son straight. The famous line from the video is, "what do you wanna do with your life." The kid's response is, "I wanna ROCK!" It is the typical rebellious teenager video, where he is allowed to fight back against all the bad things in his world, and win.

I want children to think about what they might want to do for the rest of their lives. Granted it does not have to be for the rest of their lives since people nowadays change careers quite often throughout a lifetime. I want them to at least give good thought to what makes them happy, and how that happiness can be transferred into a way of making a living.

Activity: Before the students enter your room, write on the board in big bold letters, 'WHAT DO YOU WANT TO DO WITH YOUR LIFE?'

I give them some time to write down what they want to do. Encourage them to answer as honestly as possible since it is their life that is in question. This one question will illicit stimulating conversation.

The whole point of this exercise is to encourage thought about the future, and pursue something that is worthwhile.

If you are organized, try and get your hands on the actual video and play it in class. If anything, the video is entertaining. Band: Twisted Sister, Song: We're not gonna take it.

3.7 What are you trying to say?

Write the sentence (provided below) on the board. Ask the students to write the sentence on a piece of paper, as it appears. (3 words to a line) Ask them to fill in the gaps with as many words as they wish. The sentence must make sense. Encourage the students to be as creative as possible.

Ideas to ponder: This is a way for students to understand that there may be more to an idea than first comes to mind. It may also promote the idea that not everyone thinks the same way as you do. Someone may create a very positive sentence while someone else may have created a very negative one... even though everyone starts with the same words.

Sample sentence:

Getting good grades in school is the only way to be successful in life.

Three words to one line:

Getting	good	grades
in	school	is
the	only	way
to	be	successful
in	life	

3.8 "The Precious Present"

Here is an excellent story for your students to read. This is a good ice breaker and promotes discussion right away. Have the students read the following story to themselves, and ask if they can identify the "precious present." Why is it important? Who thought the present was tangible? Does anyone dwell on the past? Is anyone waiting around for the future to happen? Is this healthy? or not? Encourage the students to come up with a list of reasons to live for today… the present.

The Precious Present *by Spencer Johnson.*

The story is about a little boy, an old man and the wisdom that comes with age.

"You have a great gift," the old man tells the boy. "It's called the precious present, and it's the best present a person can receive because anyone who receives such a gift is happy forever."

"Wow!" the little boy said. "I hope someone gives me the precious present. Maybe I'll get it for Christmas."

The old man smiled as the little boy ran off to play. The little boy was always happy, whistling, and smiling as he worked and played.

As the years passed, the boy would approach the old man and asked him again and again about the precious present. After all, the boy knew about toys. So why couldn't he figure out what the precious present was? It had to be something special, he knew, because the old man had said it would bring happiness forever.

"Is it a magical thing?" he asked.

"No," the old man said.

"A flying carpet?"

"No," the old man quietly replied.

"Sunken treasure left by pirates?" the boy asked. He was now getting older and felt uncomfortable asking. Still, he wanted to know. He *had* to know.

Finally, the boy, now a young man, became annoyed.

"You told me," he said, "that anyone who receives such a present would be happy forever. I never got such a gift as a child."

"I'm afraid you don't understand," the old man said.

"If you want me to be happy," the young man shouted, "why don't you just tell me what the precious present is?"

"And where to find it?" the old man said. "I would like to, but I do not have such power. No one does. Only you have the power to make yourself happy. Only you."

The young man left, packed his bags, and began a lifelong quest for the precious present. He looked everywhere, in caves, jungles, underneath the seas. He read books, looked in the mirror, studied the faces of other people.

But he never found the precious present.
** At this point, ask the students if they know what the Precious Present is. After small discussion, continue reading the story.

Finally, after many years, when he became an old man, it hit him what the precious present is. It is just that: The Present. Not the past and not future, but the precious present.

It's not a toy. It's not a gift.

It's the ability to live in the present tense.

This is such an important lesson for all of us today.

We are so concerned with what people say and with what people are thinking of us. We become obsessed with a loss or a failure and let it consume us. We become focused on yesterday and the mistakes of the past.

Well, yesterday's problems are just that—yesterday's. They are a done deal. There's nothing you can do about the day that's over except learn from your mistakes.

(From Pitino/Reynolds. *Success is a Choice.* 1997.)

It's easy to say you are going to live in the present, but please emphasize that it is the people who actually try are the ones who are going to succeed. Life becomes a lot more stress free and pleasant to live if we are not preoccupied with what happened yesterday let alone what might happen tomorrow. Obviously we all need to learn from our past and plan for our future, but living for the moment is paramount.

3.9 What does $1,000,000 look like?

- Ask the students to write down what they think a Million Dollars *looks* like.

- Encourage them to write down whatever comes to mind. It doesn't have to particularly make sense, but tell them that you would like an explanation of some of them.

- For example, a million dollars could look like a painting, or 5 different cars, or a gold bar, etc.

- If you want to keep going down this path, you could also ask the students what a Million Dollars would smell like, or taste like, or sound like, etc.

- This gets them to think in different terms rather than only concentrating on the visual.

More activities to ponder.

- Write a list of occupations on the board and ask the students to guess at how much that particular occupation makes annually. Doctor, lawyer, teacher, engineer, shipper/receiver, etc.

- Ask them to calculate how long it would take, in years, for that occupation to earn a million dollars. Usually the kids are surprised at how long it would actually take someone to get there.

- Now is a good time to mention taxes, expenses, bills, entertainment, and the like. *Money doesn't grow on trees!*

Use your imagination, this question conjures up many new ones!

3.10 Reasons why the English language is so hard to learn.

1. The bandage was wound around the wound.
2. The farm was used to produce produce.
3. The dump was so full that it had to refuse more refuse.
4. We must polish the Polish furniture.
5. He could lead if he would get the lead out.
6. The soldier decided to desert his dessert in the desert.
7. Since there is no time like the present, he thought it was time to present the present.
8. A bass was painted on the head of the bass drum.
9. When shot at, the dove dove into the bushes.
10. I did not object to the object.
11. I had to subject the subject to a series of tests.
12. The insurance was invalid for the invalid.
13. How can I intimate this to my most intimate friend?
14. They were too close to the door to close it.
15. The buck does funny things when the does are present.
16. A seamstress and a sewer fell down into a sewer line.
17. To help with planting, the farmer taught his sow to sow.
18. The wind was too strong to wind the sail.
19. After a number of injections my jaw got number.
20. Upon seeing the tear in the painting I shed a tear.

English is a crazy language. There is no egg in eggplant nor ham in hamburger; neither apple nor pine in pineapple. English muffins weren't invented in England or French fries in France. Sweetmeats are candies while sweetbreads, which aren't sweet, are meat. We take English for granted. But if we explore its paradoxes, we find that quicksand can work slowly, boxing rings are square and a guinea pig is neither from Guinea nor is it a pig.

And why is it that writers write but fingers don't fing, grocers don't groce and hammers don't ham? If the plural of tooth is teeth, why isn't the plural of booth beeth? One goose, 2 geese. So one moose, 2 meese? Doesn't it seem crazy that you can make amends but not one amend? If you have a bunch of odds and ends and get rid of all but one of them, what do you call it?

If teachers taught, why didn't preachers praught? If a vegetarian eats vegetables, what does a humanitarian eat? In what language do people recite at a play and play at a recital? Ship by truck and send cargo by ship? Have noses that run and feet that smell? How can a slim chance and a fat chance be the same, while a wise man and a wise guy are opposites?

You have to marvel at a language in which your house can burn up as it burns down, in which you fill in a form by filling it out and in which an alarm goes off by going on. That is why, when the stars are out, they are visible, but when the lights are out, they are invisible.

Source unknown, author unknown.

3.11 Say what?

This activity is one that you probably remember from high school. One student starts out with a story that the teacher gives him. He whispers the story into the ear of the student who is sitting in front of him. That person then tries to relay the story as best she can to the person in front of her. This goes on throughout the entire class until the last person gets the "story." The last person is asked to write down what he heard from the previous person. Now the fun begins. The first person with the correct story reads his correct version. Then the last person reads what had been relayed to him through numerous people. It is astonishing to see how the story changes.

Questions to ponder:

Why was there a difference in the story? Did every student take this exercise seriously? Why? Why not? Can everything you hear be correct? Is history believable? Why or why not?

Here is a sample story you may want to use.

A dog meandered along the sidewalk as a cat pranced on a roof top. The dog decided to scamper up the stairs and investigate a peculiar odor. As he did so, the cat bounded from one roof top to another. She was also curious.

UNIT 4
Logic

4.1 Brain Teasers

Brain Teasers are fun for everyone. I have used these on many occasions. Even if a teacher has a lesson plan for you to follow, these brain teasers are a great way to have fun with the students. They also come in handy when you might have a few minutes left in class.

UR
TIME

The answer is… You're on time.

MAN
CAMPUS

The answer is… Big man on campus.

BRERAYSAD

The answer is… Raison Bread… Rays 'in' Bread.

DECI   SION

The answer is… Split Decision.

GET GET
GET GET
NOT

The answer is… Forget me not.

BUFA

The answer is… Buffalo. The BUFA is low.

HIOISIWIEIR

The answer is… Eisenhower.

The 'I's' are in HOWER

I
GOT GOT
GOT GOT
CALL CALL

The answer is… I forgot to call.

MACHINE
+
MACHINE
+
MACHINE

The answer is… Adding machines.

P p O p D

The answer is… Two peas in a pod.

WEAR
LONG

The answer is… Long underwear.

T I D E

The answer is… Rising tide.

LITTLE LITTLE
LATE LATE

The answer is ….Too little, too late.

4.2 Riddles

1. How many letters are in the alphabet?

    Answer:
    There are 11 letters in THE ALPHABET!

2. A man walks up to you and says, "everything I say to you is a lie." Is he telling the truth or is he lying.

    Answer:
    Neither. It is a paradox and no acceptable answer exists. (*Paradox – seemingly absurd though perhaps actually well founded statement; person or thing conflicting with preconceived notion of what is reasonable or possible.*)

3. A woman has 5 children. Half of them are boys. How can this be possible?

    Answer:
    ALL the children are boys, so half are boys and the other half are boys as well.

4. A boy was at a carnival and went up to a booth where a man said to him, "If I write your exact weight on this piece of paper you have to pay me $50. If I cannot, I'll pay you $50."

    The boy looks around and sees no scale, so he figures no matter what the carny guesses, he can say that he weighs either more or less.

    In the end, the boy ended up paying the man $50. How did the man end up winning the bet?

    Answer:
    The man did exactly what he said he would and wrote "your exact weight" on a piece of paper.

5. If you were running a race and you passed the person in 2nd place, what place would you be in?

    Answer:
    You would be in 2nd place... not first place. You would have passed the 2nd place person, not the first.

6. I cannot be felt, seen or touched;
   Yet I can be found in everybody;
   My existence is always in debate;
   Yet I have my own style of music.
   What Am I?
   Answer:
   I'm a soul. Style of music: soul music

7. What are the next three letters in this riddle?
   o t t f f s s _ _ _
   Answer:
   ent... They represent the first letter of writing
   the words one through ten.

8. How can you make the following equation true by drawing only one straight line?
   5 + 5 + 5 = 550
   Answer:
   Draw a line on the first plus sign to turn it into
   a 4.
   545 + 5 = 550

9. A woman shoots her husband.
   Then she holds him under water for over 5 minutes.
   Finally she hangs him.
   But 5 minutes later they both go out together and enjoy a wonderful dinner.
   How can this be?
   Answer:
   The woman was a photographer. She shot a
   picture of her husband, developed it, and hung
   it up to dry.

10. Break it and it is better, immediately set and harder to break again. What is it?
    Answer:
    A record.

4.3 Please read the instructions.

This exercise is a wonderful activity that will make students aware of the importance of reading instructions. How many times have you asked someone to do something and realized that they completed the task incorrectly because they did not read the instructions. This happens all too often in high school classrooms.
In my experience, it can be quite frustrating to ask the students to read instructions that have been posted on the board, and then verbally answer the exact same question that is being answered on the board.

My Grade 8 Social Studies teacher, Mr. Lee, gave us a "test." We walked into class one day and were greeted with a very stern face and very succinct instructions to put our books on the floor… "YOU HAVE A TEST, and yes it counts." The only instructions Mr. Lee gave us were, "please put your name on the top right corner of your test, and please read through the test entirely before starting." After he asked if the students had any questions, they were instructed to begin. After 10 minutes had passed, he demanded that we put our pens down and hand our test forward. If the students read through the test, they would have realized that the second to last question is the key question on the test. If they followed the instructions, they would have passed the test.

Thoughts to ponder:

- What was your stress level when you first heard that you had a test? How about when you couldn't finish the test in the allotted time?

- How did you feel when you were "let off the hook" and peace and order was restored to the class?

- Will anyone remember this experience? If so, why?

YOU HAVE A TEST

NAME _____

DATE _____

INSTRUCTIONS:

Answer each question as best you can. Please read the test before you begin. Half marks will be awarded for some questions. Good luck!

1. What part of the brain is responsible for involuntary actions such as breathing and heart beat?
   _____

2. What number best represents the number of finger and toes on a "normal" human being? _____

3. Whistling is to the mouth as _____ is to the hands.

4. How should a regular North American family decide who should do those tasks that nobody wants to do? a. _____, b. _____

5. The only 4 ingredients of beer are yeast, barley,
   a. grain and bitters
   b. vinegar and cordial
   c. hops and water
   d. water and herb

6. When it is noon in Vancouver, what time is it in
   a. Auckland, New Zealand? _____
   b. Georgetown, Grand Cayman? _____
   c. New York, New York? _____
   d. Barcelona, Spain? _____

7. In Canadian Football, how many downs are there? _____.
   How many referees are on the field at one time? _____.
   Who won the 1997 Grey Cup? _____

8. True or False
   Neanderthal people inhabited the earth before Homosapien people. _____
   Multi level marketing is illegal in the United States. _____
   The estimated annual rain forest clearance worldwide is 230,000 square kilometers. _____
   Totem Poles are symbols first represented by European explorers. _____
   Satan is a figment of your imagination. _____
   Felines can have chin acne. _____
   Bill Gates is the richest man in the world. _____

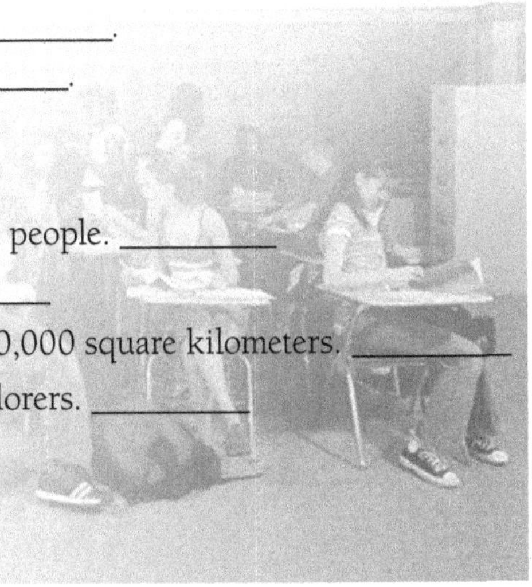

9. Define the S&P 500. _____
    _____
    _____
    _____

10. From what country does incense originate? List 5 scents.
    _____
    _____

11. Shortly before his death, Alex Haley (the author of Roots) was asked what he would suggest we do to strengthen ourselves and our society. He said, "Go out. Find the good and praise it." What wonderful opportunities for learning are inherent in that advice? _____
    _____
    _____

12. Please list the number... ok, this test is a joke. If you have read this far, know that you have passed the test. Place your pen on the top right corner of your desk. Please sit back and relax.
    _____
    _____

13. "Change will come, Change is here, Love fades out, Then love appears. Now my water's turned to wine, and these thoughts I have I now claim as mine. I'm coming home! Song Name: Reunion, Artist Name: Collective Soul. _____
    _____

4.4 Thomas Edison had a terrible batting average.

I stole this idea from my old baseball coach. I remember him saying that baseball is actually a silly game. My teammates and I were obviously curious about his statement, so we listened to what he had to say. He said, "where else in life can you do something 30% of the time and be considered good at what you do." He looked at one of us and said, "what would happen if you came home from school and announced to your parents that you got 30% on your math test." He asked, "what would happen if your father only completed 30% of his work a day?" He then asked us what a good batting average in baseball would be. One of the players said, this year Cal Ripken is hitting .347. Cal Ripken, one of the best hitters in Major League history, only hit the ball 35% of the time. 3.5 times out of 10 he would hit the ball. The point is, it's all in how you look at things. Obviously 30% on a math test is terrible, but hitting the ball 30% of the time in baseball is outstanding.

Thomas Edison fits into this category since he was a man who had a terrible "batting average." He is obviously famous for his inventions, but his track record for successes was terrible.

"There might not be a better example of persistence than Thomas Edison. A prolific inventor, Edison received 1,033 patents, including ones for the phonograph, microphone, and the incandescent electric lamp.

But think of how many failures Edison had, too. Literally thousands. To his great credit, though, Edison didn't see them as such. When reminded that he had failed something like 25,000 times while experimenting with the storage battery, Edison supposedly responded by saying, 'No, I didn't fail. I discovered 24,999 ways that the storage battery does not work.' What a marvelous outlook." (Pitino, p.192)

4.5 The GRY riddle

"Think of words ending in —GRY. Angry and hungry are two of them. There are only three words in the English language. What is the third word? The word is something that everyone uses every day. If you have listened carefully, I have already told you what it is."

Instructions:

Put this on the overhead and cover up the answer below.

Answer:

Let's take this riddle apart and solve it as a riddle. Remember, that a riddle has a trick with the words or usage of the words. The trick in this puzzle is **misdirection**. There are words here that are meant to mislead you and they do just that. The first two sentences in the puzzle have nothing to do with the question being asked: *"Think of words ending in —GRY. Angry and hungry are two of them."* Ignore these two sentences. They are there to **mislead** and **distract** you. Now, what is left is the "meat" of the riddle: *"There are only three words in* **the English language**. *What is the third word? The word is something that everyone uses every day. If you have listened carefully, I have already told you what it is."* In the phrase, **the English language**, the third word is simply the word '**language**'. There you have it! 'Language' is definitely something everyone uses every day and in the phrase "**the English language**" is the third word!

4.6 Logic questions

1. Jessica has six pairs of black gloves and six pairs of brown gloves in her drawer. In complete darkness, how many gloves must she take from the drawer in order to be sure to get a pair that match?

2. Mom, Dad, and 2 kids have come to a river, and they find a boat. It is small and can only carry one adult or 2 kids at a time. Both kids are good rowers, but how can the whole family reach the other side of the river?

3. Why can't you take a picture of a Canadian woman with curlers?

4. What is the largest possible number you can write using only 2 digits?

5. Before Mt. Everest was discovered, what was the tallest mountain in the world?

6. Because cigars cannot be entirely smoked, a hobo who collects cigar butts can make a cigar to smoke out of every 5 butts that he finds. Today, he has collected 25 cigar butts. How many cigars will he be able to smoke?

7. How many birth days does the average man have?

8. Someone at a party introduces you to your mother's only sister's husband's sister in law. He has no brothers. What do you call this lady?

9. Which weighs more, a pound of feathers or a pound of stones?

10. Two planes take off at the same exact moment. They are flying across the Atlantic. One leaves New York and is flying to Paris at 500 miles per hour. The other leaves Paris and is flying to New York at only 450 miles per hour (because of a strong head wind). Which one will be closer to Paris when they meet?

11. A carpenter was in a terrible hurry. He had to work as quickly as possible to cut a very heavy 10 foot plank into 10 equal sections. If it takes 1 minute per cut, how long will it take him to get the 10 equal pieces?

12. Why are 1898 silver dollars worth more than 1897 silver dollars?

13. What English word can have 4 of its 5 letters removed and still retain its original pronunciation?

14. Johnny's mother had three children. The first child was named April. The second child was named May. What was the third child's name?

15. In your sock drawer, you have a ratio of 5 pairs of blue socks, 4 pairs of brown socks, and 6 pairs of black socks. In complete darkness, how many socks would you need to pull out to get a matching pair of the same color?

16. How can a woman living in Alberta, legally marry 3 men, without ever getting a divorce, be widowed, or becoming legally separated?

17. A woman goes into a hardware store to buy something for her house. When asked the price, the clerk replies, "the price of one is twelve cents, the price of forty-four is twenty-four cents, and the price a hundred and forty-four is thirty-six cents. What does the woman want to buy?

18. If there are 5 apples on the counter and you take away 2, how many do you have?

19. If, having only one match, on a freezing winter day, you entered a room which contained a lamp, a kerosene heater, and a wood burning stove, which should you light first.

Logic Question Answers

1. 13. She could possibly take out 6 black left hand gloves and then 6 brown left hand gloves, the next one would have to be either the right hand or left hand match.

2. The kids row across. One comes back. An adult goes over, and the kid comes back. Both kids row across again, and one comes back. The other adult rows across and the kid comes back. Both kids row across again.

3. You can't take a picture with hair curlers, you need a camera!

4. 9^9, this is 9x9x9x9x9x9x9x9x9 or 387,420,489.

5. Mount Everest has always been the tallest mountain, even before being discovered!

6. 6, he makes 5 originals from the 25 butts he found, and after he smokes them he has 5 butts left for another cigar.

7. One, he may have many Birthdays, but only one birth day!

8. Mom

9. The answer is they both weigh the same.

10. They will both be the same distance from Paris when they meet!

11. 9 minutes. It only takes 9 cuts to get 10 equal sections.

12. $1,898.00 is one more silver dollar than $1,897.00

13. Queue

14. It has to be Johnny. He's the third child!

15. 4.

16. It's her job, she's a Justice of the Peace or a Minister.

17. House numbers.

18. You have 2 apples. There are 3 left on the counter, but you have 2.

19. The match of course!

4.7 High–Low quiz

This quiz is similar to the feature on the show the "Price is Right" where the contestants are given a price for an object and have to guess if the price is too high or too low. In this quiz you'll be given a statement of fact that has been exaggerated either too high or too low. Decide if the quoted number is too high or too low and write down your answer.

1. In Japan, women were not allowed to watch a Sumo wrestling match until **16** years ago.

2. Although a turtle is slow-moving, the "box" turtle migrates **100** miles during a single year.

3. The longest recorded life span for the "Queen" ant is **7** years.

4. The Eiffel Tower is **300** feet taller than the Washington Monument.

5. In 1993, the maker's of the game "Monopoly" printed **5** times more play money than the Bureau of Engraving and Printing did real money.

6. The tallest unicycle ever mastered was **46** feet high.

7. The King of Siam had **6,500** wives and concubines.

8. Pavarotti once received a curtain call for **2 hours and 15 minutes** after performing in a Donizetti opera.

9. In 1858, on its first day of business, the Macy's store, located in Manhattan on 6th avenue took in **$42** in sales.

10. It takes **32** muscles to frown.

11. The contact lens was invented **51** years ago.

12. The earliest jig saw puzzle was created **188** years ago.

13. The number of M&M's in a one pound bag is **425**.

14. The least populous independent country in the world had only **1,400** people there in 1993

Hi – Low Answers

1. Low. Women in Japan were allowed to watch Sumo wrestling in 1778, 221 years ago.

2. High. Box turtles typically spend their entire lives within 125 yards of their birthplace.

3. Low. An ant queen has been known to live 13 years.

4. Low. The Eiffel Tower (985') is 430 feet taller than the Washington Monument (555').

5. High. The maker's of the game "Monopoly" printed $21.5 billion in 1993. The Bureau of Engraving and Printing printed $104.3 billion in 1993.

6. Low. The tallest unicycle ever mastered was 101' 9" high. It was ridden a distance of 376' in Las Vegas by Steve McPeak with the aid of a safety wire suspended by an overhead crane.

7. Low. The King of Siam (King Mongkut) had 9,000 wives and concubines.

8. High. Pavarotti once received 165 curtain calls, lasting 1 hour and 7 minutes after performing at the German Opera house in Berlin.

9. High. The original Macy's took in just $11.06 on its first day of business.

10. Low. It takes 47 muscles to frown. To smile it only takes 17 muscles.

11. Low. The first contact lens was designed in 1887 by a German glassblower 112 years ago. Plastic lenses came about 50 years later.

12. Low. The earliest written reference to jig saw puzzles was in 1763, 236 years ago.

13. Low. The average number of M&M's in a one pound bag is 521.

14. High. Vatican City, the least populous independent country in the world had a population of 800 in 1993.

4.8 There are always 2 sides to every story.

This activity poses a question. Why are there always two sides to every story? I got the idea for this activity by watching too much "Law and Order" on TV. Episode after episode, lawyers would argue about the same event, but would have two totally different opinions of the actual events. It struck me that know matter what had actually occurred; one could legitimately present information that could sway a jury in their favor. An obvious real life example is the OJ Simpson trial. There are people who adamantly believe that OJ Simpson is a double murderer. There are obviously other people who think he is an innocent man who has been framed by a racist police department.

- Ask the students to write down an experience in their own lives where they truly believed that they were correct.

- Once you have given them enough time to do so, ask them to pass their sheet of paper to a partner or friend.

- Ask that person to try and come up with another side to that story. Encourage them to be as realistic as possible.

- Have them try to explain as best they can. Encourage the students to ask questions about the original story with their partner.

- Once they have completed this, you can select a few to review.

- This exercise may be exaggerated, but the point is to show that sometimes, two people can have totally different opinions about the same event, and in some cases, both be right!

4.9 Funny questions that make you go huh?

1. Why do we say something is out of whack? What's a whack?

2. If a pig loses its voice, is it disgruntled?

3. When someone asks you, a penny for your thoughts, and you put your two cents in, what happens to the other penny? Or do you get change?

4. Why is the man or woman who invests all your money called a broker?

5. Why is a person who plays the piano called a pianist but a person who drives a race car not called a racist?

6. Why are a wise man and a wise guy opposites?

7. Why do overlook and oversee mean opposite things?

8. Why isn't 11 pronounced onety one?

9. If lawyers are disbarred and clergymen defrocked, doesn't it follow that electricians can be delighted, musicians denoted, cowboys deranged, models deposed, tree surgeons debarked, and dry cleaners depressed?

10. If Fed Ex and UPS were to merge, would they call it Fed UP?

11. Do Lipton Tea employees take coffee breaks?

12. No one ever says "It's only a game," when their team is winning.

13. Ever wonder what the speed of lightning would be if it didn't zigzag?

14. If a cow laughed, would milk come out her nose?

15. Whatever happened to preparations A through G?

16. If olive oil comes from olives, where does baby oil come from?

4.10 The missing dollar riddle

Three buddies check into a motel for the night and the clerk tells them the bill is $30, payable in advance. So, they each pay the clerk $10 and go to their room. A few minutes later, the clerk realizes he has made an error and overcharged the trio by $5. He asks the bellhop to return $5 to the 3 friends who had just checked in. The bellhop sees this as an opportunity to make $2 as he reasons that the three friends would have a tough time dividing $5 evenly among them; so he decides to tell them that the clerk made a mistake of only $3, giving a dollar back to each of the friends. He pockets the left-over $2 and goes home for the day! Now, each of the three friends gets a dollar back, thus they each paid $9 for the room which is a total of $27 for the night. We know the bellhop pocketed $2 and adding that to the $27, you get $29, not $30 which was originally spent. Where did the other dollar go?

SOLUTION

The facts in this riddle are clear: There is an initial $30 charge. It should have been $25, so $5 must be returned and accounted for. $3 is given to the 3 buddies, $2 is kept by the bellhop—there you have the $5. The trick to this riddle is that the addition and subtraction are done at the wrong times to misdirect your thinking—and quite successfully for most. Each of the 3 buddies did indeed pay $9, not $10, and as far as the friends are concerned, they paid $27 for the night. But we know that the clerk will tell us that they were charged only $25 and when you add the $3 returned with the $2 kept by the bellhop, you come up with $30.

4.11 More crazy questions

1. On a standard traffic light, is the green on the top or bottom?
2. What 2 letters don't appear on the telephone dial?
3. What 2 #'s on the telephone dial don't have letters by them?
4. When you walk does your left arm swing w/ your right or left leg?
5. How many matches are in a standard pack?
6. What is the lowest # on the FM dial?
7. Which way does water go down the drain, clockwise or counter-clockwise?
8. Which way does a "no smoking" sign's slash run?
9. Which side of a woman's blouse are the buttons on?
10. Which way do fans rotate?
11. How many sides does a stop sign have?
12. Do books have even # pages on the right or left side?
13. How many lug nuts are on a standard car wheel?
14. How many sides are there on a standard pencil?
15. Sleepy, Happy, Sneezy, Grumpy, Dopey, Doc. Who's missing?
16. How many hot dog buns are in a standard package?
17. On which side of a venetian blind is the cord that adjusts the opening between the slats?
18. How many curves are in a standard paper clip?
19. Does a merry-go-round turn clockwise or counter-clockwise?

Answers on reverse

ANSWERS:

1. Bottom
2. Q, Z
3. 1, 0
4. Left
5. 20
6. 88
7. Counter-clockwise (unless you happen to be south of the equator)
8. Towards the bottom right
9. Right
10. Clockwise as you look at it
11. 8
12. Left
13. 5
14. 6
15. Bashful
16. 6
17. Left
18. 3
19. Counter-clockwise

4.12 Confusing questions

1. Who was the first person to look at a cow and say, "I think I'll squeeze these dangly things here, and drink whatever comes out."

2. Who was the first person to say "See that chicken there,... I'm gonna eat the next thing that comes outta its butt."

3. Why do toasters always have a setting that burns the toast to a horrible crisp?

4. Why is there a light in the fridge and not in the freezer?

5. If Jimmy cracks corn and no one cares, why is there a song about him?

6. Can a hearse carrying a corpse drive in the carpool lane?

7. If the professor on Gilligan's Island can make a radio out of coconut, why can't he fix a hole in a boat?

8. Why do people point to their wrist when asking for the time, but don't point to their crotch when they ask where the bathroom is?

9. Why does Goofy stand erect while Pluto remains on all fours? They're both dogs!

10. What do you call male ballerinas?

11. If quizzes are quizzical, what are tests?

12. If corn oil is made from corn, and vegetable oil is made from vegetables, then what is baby oil made from?

13. If electricity comes from electrons, does morality come from morons?

14. Why do the Alphabet song and Twinkle, Twinkle Little Star have the same tune?

15. Does pushing the elevator button more than once make it arrive faster?

4.13 Do you know the answer?

1. How many batters does a pitcher face in a perfect game?
2. How long did the Hundred Years War last?
3. Which country makes panama hats?
4. What is a camel's hair brush made of?
5. How long did the Thirty Years War last?
6. What starts with "e" ends with "e" and contains only one letter?
7. Which room has no door, no window, no floors and no roof?
8. What do we all put off until tomorrow?
9. What has eyes but can't see?
10. What is hard to beat?
11. What is too much for one, enough for two, but nothing at all for three?
12. What is the difference between the teacher and a cashier?
13. What do men want the least on their hands?
14. This you should always keep—no one else wants it.
15. What is the end to which we all like to come?
16. It wasn't my sister, nor my brother, but still was the child of my father and mother. Who was it?
17. What is everyone in the world doing at the same time?
18. What can be measured, but has no length, width or height?
19. Why is the world like a faulty jig saw puzzle?
20. What do you break by saying just one word?
21. What flies when it's on and floats when it's off?
22. What has a big mouth, yet never speaks?
23. What question can you never answer "yes" to?
24. What can't you see that is always before you?
25. What can you hold without ever touching or using your hands?
26. Which 3 Canadian cities always have a white Christmas?
27. What famous landmark is constantly moving backwards?
28. Which 4 Canadian provinces have native origins?
29. In what school do you learn to greet people?
30. What year was the Canadian National Anthem written?

Answers:

1. 27
2. 116 years 1337-1453
3. Ecuador
4. squirrel fur
5. 30 years 1618-1648
6. an envelope
7. a mushroom
8. our clothes
9. potatoes
10. a drum with a hole in it
11. a secret
12. one tills the mind and the other minds the till
13. handcuffs
14. your temper
15. dividend
16. the person speaking
17. growing older
18. temperature
19. because peace is missing
20. silence
21. a feather
22. a jar
23. are you asleep?
24. the future
25. your breath
26. Quebec City, Winnipeg, Saskatoon
27. Niagara Falls
28. Quebec–narrow passage or strait, Ontario–beautiful lakes/waters, Manitoba–strait of the spirit, Saskatchewan–swift flowing river.
29. Hi school
30. 1908

4.14 Analogies

analogy n. correspondence or partial similarity of things;
reasoning from parallel cases. (The Oxford Dictionary)

1. Complete is to entire as usual is to
    _____.

2. Cry is to sob as job is to
    _____.

3. Band is trumpeter as network is to
    _____.

4. Stubborn is to donkey as wise is to
    _____.

5. Plenty is to scarce as graceful is to
    _____.

6. Snow is to flake as sand is to
    _____.

7. Eye is to pupil as cherry is to
    _____.

8. Sunday is to week as October is to
    _____.

9. Busy is to idle as simple is to
    _____.

10. Centimeter is to length as kilogram is to
    _____.

ANSWERS:

1. Ordinary   6. Grain

2. Chore   7. Pit

3. Broadcaster   8. Years

4. Owl   9. Difficult

5. Awkward   10. Weight

UNIT 5
Quotations

5.1 Vince Lombardi

I think it is always fun to dissect famous quotations from famous people. Vince Lombardi was a successful football coach in the NFL from 1959–1969, but it doesn't matter who the person is, because you can always learn something from successful people. From my experience, the majority of the students that I taught had no idea who Vince Lombardi was, but it was fun to show the quotes and have the students guess what he did to make him famous. You and your students will be amazed at how these quotations can relate to an abundance of topics.

Vincent T. "Vince" Lombardi

"They call it coaching, but it is teaching. You do not just tell them it is so. You show them the reasons why it is so, and then you repeat and repeat until they are convinced, until they know."

"Don't ask questions you can answer yourself."

"Coaches who can outline plays on a blackboard are a dime a dozen. The ones who win get inside their players and motivate them."

"To be a good coach, you have to be the opposite of what you feel. When your team is going bad, you want to get on their ass but that's when everybody else is on their ass. Their family, their friends, the fans, the media, the guy in the grocery store. That's when you need to pat them on the back, to tell them to just keep working hard and everything will be all right. Conversely, when everything is going good, you don't have to pat them on the back because everybody else is. That's when you have to be tough."

"The greatest glory is not in never falling but in rising every time we fall."

"Teams do not go physically stale. They go mentally stale."

"No leader, however great, can long continue unless he wins battles. The battle decides all."

5.2 Famous quotations

Ask not what your country can do for you… ask what you can do for your country.
—*Former President of the USA John F. Kennedy*

You ain't nothing but a hound dog, Cry'in all the time. You ain't never caught a rabbit and you ain't no friend of mine.
—*Elvis Presley*

Can't we all just get along?
—*Rodney King, victim of a brutal police attack*

A woman needs a man like a fish needs a bicycle.
—*Bono of U2*

Imagination is more important than knowledge. Knowledge is limited. Imagination encircles the world.
—*Albert Einstein*

Citius, Altius, Fortius… Faster, Higher, Stronger
—*Olympic Motto*

I have a dream!…
—*Martin Luther King Jr.*

Float like a butterfly and sting like a bee.
—*Muhammad Ali*

One small step for man, one giant leap for mankind.
—*Neil Armstrong, First man to walk on the moon*

It's kind of fun to do the impossible.
—*Walt Disney*

Following the light of the sun, we left the old world.
—*Christopher Columbus*

Live as if you were to die tomorrow. Learn as if you were to live forever.
—*Mahatma Gandhi*

The leader of genius must have the ability to make different opponents appear as if they belonged to one category.
—*Adolf Hitler*

God have mercy on the man who doubts what he's sure of.
—*Bruce Springsteen*

5.3 Yogi Berraisms

"Yogi Berra has been credited with some of recent histories most peculiar as well as influential quotations. His simple yet thought provoking sayings have been the topic of many books, valedictory speeches and corporate business meetings. Yogi Berra is one of America's most beloved baseball heroes of all time, known as much for his wit and humor as he is for his exploits with the New York Yankees for whom he was a 3 time MVP and Hall of Famer."

(When You Come to a Fork in the Road, Take It!)

These sayings can jump start a discussion on what they actually mean. Even if the students don't know who Yogi Berra is, they can still get a laugh out of his odd take on life. In some ways, these "life lessons" will encourage students to take a look at their own lives and hopefully reflect on Berra's truthful yet strange perception of the world.

"When you come to a fork in the road, take it."

"It's never happened in World Series history, and it hasn't happened since."

"Nobody did nothin' to nobody."

"Slump? I ain't in no slump. I just ain't hitting."

"We have a good time together, even when we're not together."

"Public speaking is one of the best things I hate."

"He's learning me all his experience."

"If you don't have a bullpen, you got nothing."

"If people don't want to come out to the park, nobody's going to stop them."

"You can't win all the time. There are guys out there who are better than you."

"Don't get me right, I'm just asking."

"If you don't know where you're going, you might not get there."

"90% of the game is half mental."

"Why buy good luggage? You only use it when you travel."

"You can observe a lot by watching."

"It's déjà vu all over again."

"We make too many wrong mistakes."

"Little League Baseball is a good thing because it keeps the parents off the street and the kids out of the house."

"A nickel ain't worth a dime anymore."

"It ain't over 'till it's over."

"It gets late early out here."

"If you can't imitate him, don't copy him."

"Nobody goes there anymore. It's too crowded."

"So I'm ugly. So what? I don't hit with my face."

"There is always some kid who may be seeing me for the first time or last time. I owe him my best."

"Only in America."

5.4 Clichés

The world is full of clichés. Everyone uses them to a certain degree throughout their lives. Sometimes these clichés can be very easy to understand, yet other times these little sayings can be very confusing. (Being from Vancouver, the city is a very multicultural society. Many people from different countries have difficulty understanding North American clichés. I've encountered many blank faces when trying to teach English to students who were born and raised in Asia.) In this activity we can engage the students in recognizing what a cliché is, when it is appropriate to use, and ultimately what they mean. This can be a fun exercise for the students. The class can be split up into groups of 2 or 3 and each cliché can be presented on the overhead projector one at a time. Ask the students to write down what they think the cliché actually means and give an example of an appropriate time to use it.

Questions to Ponder:

Are the same clichés used throughout the world? Why/why not? Who do you think came up with these in the first place? Can you think of more clichés? List 10. Does anyone have a cliché from a different culture that they can share with the class?

To go postal

For the life of me

It's a jungle out there

Off the wall

You said a mouthful

Get on a high horse

One slice short of a loaf

Follow your heart

Put the moves on (a girl or a guy)

As nervous as a hooker in church

Life sucks, then you die!

All for one and one for all

Happier than a pig in mud

Looked down his nose

It's on the Fritz

If you can't beat'em, join them

Laughing all the way to the bank

No blood, no foul

As easy as shooting fish in a barrel

Rubs me the wrong way

Bag of Tricks

Here is a list of items that you should carry in your Bag of Tricks:

Eraser	fastfood ketchup, vinegar, salt, pepper
Crayons	rubber chicken
Pens	wig
Pencils	headphones
Poker chips	pictures for 2.2 First impressions
Playing cards	measurement conversion chart
Other card games	maps
A book of matches	magnifying glass
Candy	bottle opener
Buzzers	cork screw
Key chain	nerf football
Fake money	Sports Illustrated
Bouncy balls	People magazine
Marbles	fork
Small plastic shot glasses	spoon
Videos (sports, music, car crashes)	chop sticks
Pop bottle	Prizes
Coins	Plastic bags
Paper clips	Magnets
Calculator	Tape measure
Stickers	Swiss army knife
Kitchen towel	All purpose screw driver
Recycled paper	Push pins
Hi liters	Glue stick
White out	Silly hat
Drum sticks	Watch
Tennis ball	Dice
Dominoes	

References

Berra, Yogi. (2001) *When You Come to a Fork in the Road, Take It,*
New York, Hyperion.

Carlson, Richard. (1997) *Don't Sweat the Small Stuff, It's all Small Stuff,*
New York, Hyperion.

Pitino, Rick. (1997) *Success is a Choice,*
New York. Broadway Books.

Townsend, Tony and George Otero. (1999) *The Global Classroom: Activities to engage students in third millennium schools,*
Victoria Australia, Hawker Brownlow.

www.quoteland.com

www.miss-charming.com

www.cubiclecommando.com

www.justriddlesandmore.com

www.afunzone.com

www.amusingfacts.com

*some information is assumed to be in the public domain

Printed in the United States
By Bookmasters